I SPY PASSOVER!

With Coloring Pages

This Book Belongs To:

_____

HAPPY PASSOVER

Coperything By Joshua Tigger Publishing

TEST COLOR PAGE

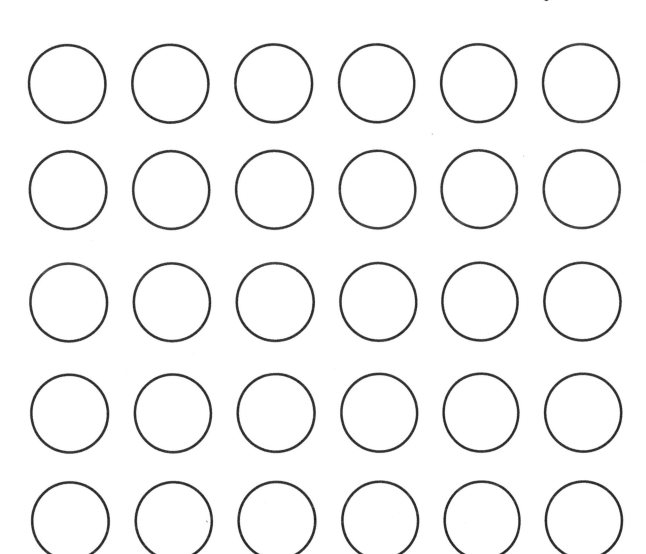

SINGLE-SIDED PAGES - EVERY IMAGE IS PLACED ON ITS OWN
PAGE TO REDUCE THE BLEED-THROUGH PROBLEM FOUND IN
OTHER COLORING BOOKS

JOSHUA TIGGER PUBLISHING

I Spy with my little eye something starting with:

SINGLE-SIDED PAGES - EVERY IMAGE IS PLACED ON ITS OWN
PAGE TO REDUCE THE BLEED-THROUGH PROBLEM FOUND IN
OTHER COLORING BOOKS

JOSHUA TIGGER PUBLISHING

M is for

MATZAH

SINGLE-SIDED PAGES - EVERY IMAGE IS PLACED ON ITS OWN
PAGE TO REDUCE THE BLEED-THROUGH PROBLEM FOUND IN
OTHER COLORING BOOKS

JOSHUA TIGGER PUBLISHING

I Spy with my little eye something starting with:

SINGLE-SIDED PAGES - EVERY IMAGE IS PLACED ON ITS OWN
PAGE TO REDUCE THE BLEED-THROUGH PROBLEM FOUND IN
OTHER COLORING BOOKS

JOSHUA TIGGER PUBLISHING

B is for

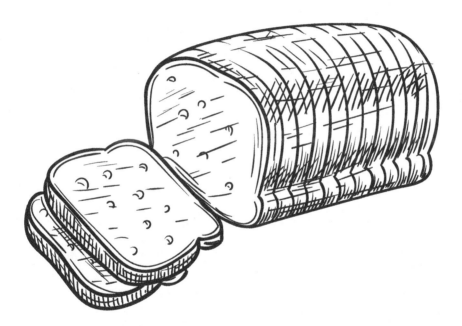

BREAD
CHOMETZ

SINGLE-SIDED PAGES - EVERY IMAGE IS PLACED ON ITS OWN
PAGE TO REDUCE THE BLEED-THROUGH PROBLEM FOUND IN
OTHER COLORING BOOKS

JOSHUA TIGGER PUBLISHING

I Spy with my little eye something starting with:

P

SINGLE-SIDED PAGES - EVERY IMAGE IS PLACED ON ITS OWN
PAGE TO REDUCE THE BLEED-THROUGH PROBLEM FOUND IN
OTHER COLORING BOOKS

JOSHUA TIGGER PUBLISHING

P is for

PHARAOH

SINGLE-SIDED PAGES - EVERY IMAGE IS PLACED ON ITS OWN
PAGE TO REDUCE THE BLEED-THROUGH PROBLEM FOUND IN
OTHER COLORING BOOKS

JOSHUA TIGGER PUBLISHING

I Spy with my little eye something starting with:

E

לא תרצח | אנוכי ה'
לא תנאף | לא יהיה
לא תגנב | לא תשא
לא תענה | זכור את
לא תחמד | בבד את

SINGLE-SIDED PAGES - EVERY IMAGE IS PLACED ON ITS OWN
PAGE TO REDUCE THE BLEED-THROUGH PROBLEM FOUND IN
OTHER COLORING BOOKS

JOSHUA TIGGER PUBLISHING

E is for

Elijah Cup

ELIJAH'S CUP

SINGLE-SIDED PAGES - EVERY IMAGE IS PLACED ON ITS OWN
PAGE TO REDUCE THE BLEED-THROUGH PROBLEM FOUND IN
OTHER COLORING BOOKS

JOSHUA TIGGER PUBLISHING

I Spy with my little eye something starting with:

SINGLE-SIDED PAGES - EVERY IMAGE IS PLACED ON ITS OWN
PAGE TO REDUCE THE BLEED-THROUGH PROBLEM FOUND IN
OTHER COLORING BOOKS

JOSHUA TIGGER PUBLISHING

F is for

FROG

SINGLE-SIDED PAGES - EVERY IMAGE IS PLACED ON ITS OWN
PAGE TO REDUCE THE BLEED-THROUGH PROBLEM FOUND IN
OTHER COLORING BOOKS

JOSHUA TIGGER PUBLISHING

I Spy with my little eye something starting with:

SINGLE-SIDED PAGES - EVERY IMAGE IS PLACED ON ITS OWN
PAGE TO REDUCE THE BLEED-THROUGH PROBLEM FOUND IN
OTHER COLORING BOOKS

JOSHUA TIGGER PUBLISHING

M is for

MOSES

SINGLE-SIDED PAGES - EVERY IMAGE IS PLACED ON ITS OWN
PAGE TO REDUCE THE BLEED-THROUGH PROBLEM FOUND IN
OTHER COLORING BOOKS

JOSHUA TIGGER PUBLISHING

I Spy with my little eye something starting with:

S

SINGLE-SIDED PAGES - EVERY IMAGE IS PLACED ON ITS OWN
PAGE TO REDUCE THE BLEED-THROUGH PROBLEM FOUND IN
OTHER COLORING BOOKS

JOSHUA TIGGER PUBLISHING

S is for

SEDER PLATE

SINGLE-SIDED PAGES - EVERY IMAGE IS PLACED ON ITS OWN
PAGE TO REDUCE THE BLEED-THROUGH PROBLEM FOUND IN
OTHER COLORING BOOKS

JOSHUA TIGGER PUBLISHING

I Spy with my little eye something starting with:

SINGLE-SIDED PAGES - EVERY IMAGE IS PLACED ON ITS OWN
PAGE TO REDUCE THE BLEED-THROUGH PROBLEM FOUND IN
OTHER COLORING BOOKS

JOSHUA TIGGER PUBLISHING

P is for

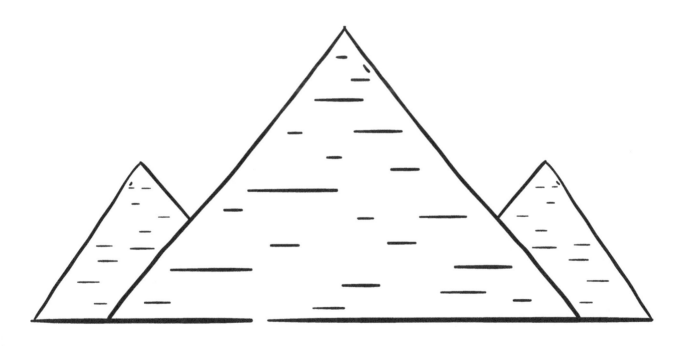

PYRAMIDS

SINGLE-SIDED PAGES - EVERY IMAGE IS PLACED ON ITS OWN
PAGE TO REDUCE THE BLEED-THROUGH PROBLEM FOUND IN
OTHER COLORING BOOKS

JOSHUA TIGGER PUBLISHING

I Spy with my little eye something starting with:

SINGLE-SIDED PAGES - EVERY IMAGE IS PLACED ON ITS OWN
PAGE TO REDUCE THE BLEED-THROUGH PROBLEM FOUND IN
OTHER COLORING BOOKS

JOSHUA TIGGER PUBLISHING

T is for

TAMBOURINE

SINGLE-SIDED PAGES - EVERY IMAGE IS PLACED ON ITS OWN
PAGE TO REDUCE THE BLEED-THROUGH PROBLEM FOUND IN
OTHER COLORING BOOKS

JOSHUA TIGGER PUBLISHING

I Spy with my little eye something starting with:

W

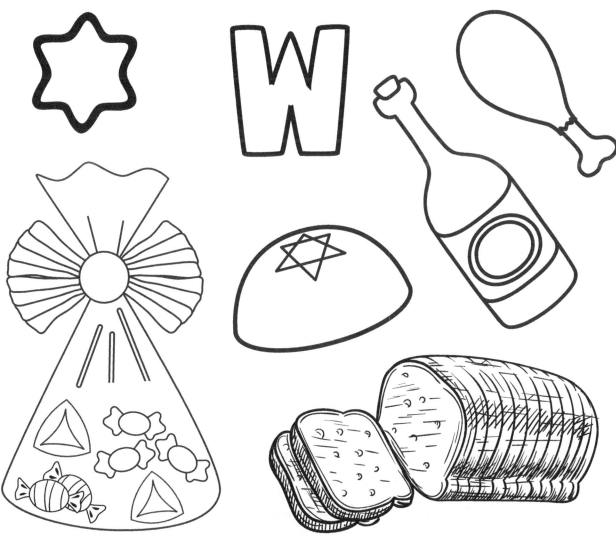

SINGLE-SIDED PAGES - EVERY IMAGE IS PLACED ON ITS OWN
PAGE TO REDUCE THE BLEED-THROUGH PROBLEM FOUND IN
OTHER COLORING BOOKS

JOSHUA TIGGER PUBLISHING

SINGLE-SIDED PAGES - EVERY IMAGE IS PLACED ON ITS OWN
PAGE TO REDUCE THE BLEED-THROUGH PROBLEM FOUND IN
OTHER COLORING BOOKS

JOSHUA TIGGER PUBLISHING

I Spy with my little eye something starting with:

C

SINGLE-SIDED PAGES - EVERY IMAGE IS PLACED ON ITS OWN PAGE TO REDUCE THE BLEED-THROUGH PROBLEM FOUND IN OTHER COLORING BOOKS

JOSHUA TIGGER PUBLISHING

C is for

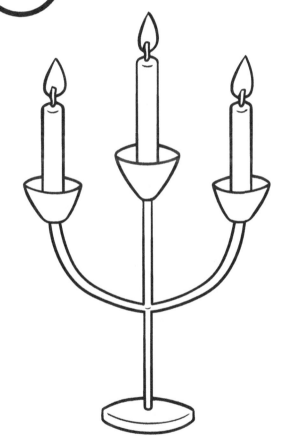

CANDLESTICK

SINGLE-SIDED PAGES - EVERY IMAGE IS PLACED ON ITS OWN
PAGE TO REDUCE THE BLEED-THROUGH PROBLEM FOUND IN
OTHER COLORING BOOKS

JOSHUA TIGGER PUBLISHING

I Spy with my little eye something starting with:

SINGLE-SIDED PAGES - EVERY IMAGE IS PLACED ON ITS OWN
PAGE TO REDUCE THE BLEED-THROUGH PROBLEM FOUND IN
OTHER COLORING BOOKS

JOSHUA TIGGER PUBLISHING

H is for

HAGGADAH

SINGLE-SIDED PAGES - EVERY IMAGE IS PLACED ON ITS OWN
PAGE TO REDUCE THE BLEED-THROUGH PROBLEM FOUND IN
OTHER COLORING BOOKS

JOSHUA TIGGER PUBLISHING

I Spy with my little eye something starting with:

SINGLE-SIDED PAGES - EVERY IMAGE IS PLACED ON ITS OWN
PAGE TO REDUCE THE BLEED-THROUGH PROBLEM FOUND IN
OTHER COLORING BOOKS

JOSHUA TIGGER PUBLISHING

P is for

PITCHER

SINGLE-SIDED PAGES - EVERY IMAGE IS PLACED ON ITS OWN
PAGE TO REDUCE THE BLEED-THROUGH PROBLEM FOUND IN
OTHER COLORING BOOKS

JOSHUA TIGGER PUBLISHING

I Spy with my little eye something starting with:

G

SINGLE-SIDED PAGES - EVERY IMAGE IS PLACED ON ITS OWN
PAGE TO REDUCE THE BLEED-THROUGH PROBLEM FOUND IN
OTHER COLORING BOOKS

JOSHUA TIGGER PUBLISHING

G is for

GIFT

SINGLE-SIDED PAGES - EVERY IMAGE IS PLACED ON ITS OWN
PAGE TO REDUCE THE BLEED-THROUGH PROBLEM FOUND IN
OTHER COLORING BOOKS

JOSHUA TIGGER PUBLISHING

I Spy with my little eye something starting with:

SINGLE-SIDED PAGES - EVERY IMAGE IS PLACED ON ITS OWN
PAGE TO REDUCE THE BLEED-THROUGH PROBLEM FOUND IN
OTHER COLORING BOOKS

JOSHUA TIGGER PUBLISHING

C is for

CUP

SINGLE-SIDED PAGES - EVERY IMAGE IS PLACED ON ITS OWN
PAGE TO REDUCE THE BLEED-THROUGH PROBLEM FOUND IN
OTHER COLORING BOOKS

JOSHUA TIGGER PUBLISHING

I Spy with my little eye something starting with:

SINGLE-SIDED PAGES - EVERY IMAGE IS PLACED ON ITS OWN
PAGE TO REDUCE THE BLEED-THROUGH PROBLEM FOUND IN
OTHER COLORING BOOKS

JOSHUA TIGGER PUBLISHING

S is for

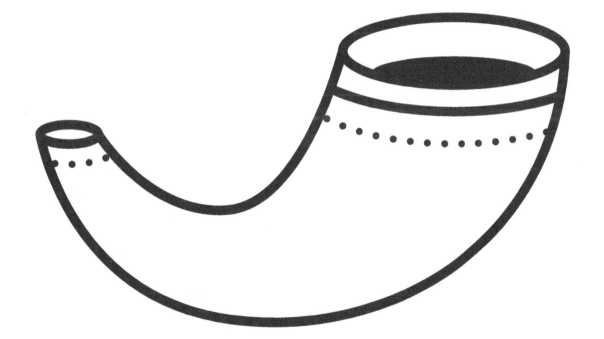

SHOFAR

SINGLE-SIDED PAGES - EVERY IMAGE IS PLACED ON ITS OWN
PAGE TO REDUCE THE BLEED-THROUGH PROBLEM FOUND IN
OTHER COLORING BOOKS

JOSHUA TIGGER PUBLISHING

I AM VERY GRATEFUL YOU PURCHASED THIS BOOK. I HOPE YOU AND YOUR CHILD SPEND AN UNFORGETTABLE TIME HAVING FUN AND LEARNING TOGETHER FROM THIS BOOK.

IF YOU CAN, I WOULD BE EXTREMELY GRATEFUL IF YOU COULD LEAVE A REVIEW ON AMAZON. WE ARE A SMALL FAMILY BUSINESS AND DEPEND ON REVIEWS TO REACH MORE FAMILIES.

THANK YOU AGAIN FOR YOUR PURCHASE AND YOUR TRUST. I HOPE YOU ENJOY YOUR BOOK AND HAVE A GREAT TIME WITH YOUR FAMILY

HAPPY PASSOVER!

WE HOPE THE BOOK HAS MET YOUR EXPECTATIONS, IF YOU FOUND ANY MISTAKES IN THE BOOK PLEASE CONTACT US BY EMAIL, AND WE WILL CORRECT THEM AS SOON AS POSSIBLE.

office.dannyd@gmail.com

INDEPENDENTLY PUBLISHED

Joshua Tigger Publishing

ILLUSTRATIONS:
HTTPS://WWW.FREEPIK.COM/

Made in the USA
Las Vegas, NV
08 April 2024

88427241R00039